TALKABOUT
Air

TALKABOUT
Air

Text: Angela Webb
Photography: Chris Fairclough

Franklin Watts
London/New York/Sydney/Toronto

©1986 Franklin Watts

First published in Great Britain by

Franklin Watts
12a Golden Square
London W1

First published in the USA by

Franklin Watts Inc
387 Park Avenue South
New York 10016

ISBN: UK edition 0 86313 475 0

ISBN: US edition 0–531–10369–2
Library of Congress
Catalog Card No: 87–50234

Editor: Ruth Thomson
Design: Edward Kinsey
Additional Photographs: Zefa
Heather Angel

Typesetting: Keyspools Ltd
Printed in Italy

About this book

This book has been written for young children—in the playgroup, school and at home.

Its aim is to increase children's awareness of the world around them and to promote thought and discussion about topics of scientific interest.

The book draws on examples from a child's own environment. The activities and experiments suggested are simple enough for children to conduct themselves, with only a little help from an adult, using objects and materials which will be familiar to them.

Children will gain most from the book if the book is used together with practical activities. Such experiences will help to consolidate knowledge and also suggest new ideas for further exploration and experimentation.

The themes explored in this book include:

Air exists, even though you cannot see it.
Wind is air moving.
Air fills space.
Air has weight.
Air is buoyant.
Air is essential to life.

Where is air?

It's all around you.

You can feel air moving
when it's windy.

You can feel it
blowing against your face,
billowing your clothes

and tugging your hair.

You cannot see air,
but you can see what it does.

What is making
these flags move

and making these trees
wave and sway?

What is swirling the smoke?

You can make air move.

What happens
when you fan
yourself?

What can you feel
when you run fast or cycle?

Take a deep breath.
You are sucking
in air.

When you hold
your breath,
your chest is full
of air, just like
a blown-up balloon.

Now breathe out.
You are blowing
out air.
How does your
chest feel now?

When you breathe out on a cold day, you can see your warm breath coming out into the cold air.

Many things which look empty
are really full of air.

You can blow into things.
What makes the water-wings firm
to touch?

These children are filling balloons with air.

What happens if they let one go?

Sometimes air is strong enough
to hold you up . . . . .

Can we measure the weight of air?

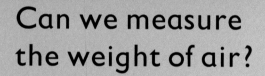

Which of these things do you think is likely to be heavier than the blown up balloon?

Many things can float
in air.

Try this experiment.
What do you notice
about the way
these things fall?

Some things fall
straight down,
others fall more slowly.
Why do you think this is?

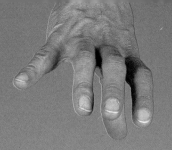

Drop a sheet of paper.
How does it fall?
What can you do to it
to make it fall more quickly?

Now drop a folded handkerchief.
If you open it out
does it fall in the same way?

Could we live in a world
without air?